Defining Autism
From The Heart

From Nonverbal to National Speaker

Kerry Magro, M.A.

ISBN: 0615818102
ISBN-13: 978-0615818108

DISCLAIMER

Throughout this book, I often switch between using terms such as "have autism" and "autistic." This is not to confuse anyone. I rarely notice when I switch between both terms in my writing. I know there are two sides of this debate in the autism community, and I respect both sides' opinions. My main focus here is not to add to this debate but to let you into a part of who I am through my writing.

DEDICATION

This book is dedicated to all the autistic individuals out there and their families who are trying to progress and grow each and everyday. It's important to understand like anyone else we all have strengths and weaknesses. For those who keep fighting the good fight on our behalf this is my way of saying thank you. Even if you don't see it sometimes you are making a difference everyday! Keep it up!

CONTENTS

ACKNOWLEDGMENTS

There are so many people I'd like to thank for making not only this book possible but for making my life truly amazing.

First I have to give credit to my parents, Bob Magro and Suzanne Mack-Magro, who have loved and supported me throughout my life. You have shown me what it is to get to the next level in my life and for that I'm eternally grateful.

This book also wouldn't have been possible without the amazing contributions of our extended families, my "other brother" Pravin Jadhav and my doctor Dr. Barney Softness of West End Pediatrics in New York. Because of Dr. Softness we were referred to Dr. Margaret Hertzig from Cornell Medical Hospital who diagnosed me with autism and they both have had a big impact in my overall development.

I would like to give special shout outs to Bill O'Dea, David Fischer, Joe Doria and Carl Gargiulo who have played integral parts in my journey to this point.

A special thank you goes to NJ Senator Robert Menendez, who was a key sponsor in the Senate of the Combating Autism Reauthorization Act, (CARA) and my friend.

Finally, I wouldn't be here without the rest of my family and friends who have contributed and accepted me for who I am. Thank you all so much for everything!

INTRODUCTION

When I was a kid, I had no idea how much work I was going to have to go through to get to where I am today. For all intents and purposes, for most of my childhood, I was working a nine-to-five "job" without the checks. In fact, my parents most of the time were paying the checks, so I could go to work. This isn't your typical work though that you do for a company but work that you do to give yourself a shot at a future.

This job was necessary because of something that has been a part of me, for better or for worse, and that is autism. When I was only four, I was diagnosed at Hackensack Medical Center in New Jersey with Pervasive Developmental Disorder- Not Otherwise Specified, (PDD-NOS) a form of autism. The diagnoses did not paint an optimistic picture for my future. Contrary to that my future has included graduating college, getting a Master of Arts degree in Strategic Communications, living independently and much much more.

You see autism is very much a mixed bag. It is a complex neurodevelopmental disorder. Today countless individuals and organizations around the world are trying to learn more about autism in order to help their loved ones' advance every day.

Today, one in 88 children are diagnosed with autism while back when I was diagnosed the numbers were closer to 1 in every 1,000!! These numbers are staggering, and if recent history is any indication, it only looks to increase. 500,000 children will become adults with autism in the next decade, and we have to be ready for them.

I really hope we do make a difference for these individuals. Growing up I dealt with countless challenges. One of the earliest challenges was being nonverbal (mild articulation delay) until I was two and a half. I faced severe communication and verbal delays in both receptive and expressive language. (Moderate to Severe Receptive and Expressive Language Disorder) Plus I had auditory processing issues, and sensory integration dysfunction. I was always a step behind my peers in these areas. In addition to the verbal and motor skill delays, (Somatosensory Processing Disorder with gross and fine motor dyspraxia) I had retention issues, problems with reading, (Scattered pre-academic achievement) twirling myself around, some flapping (Mild adaptive behavior delay), and repeating things (echolalia): all of which truly held me back for some time. My inability to communicate effectively and appropriately left me with a great deal of emotional issues, which made my day-to-day behavior unpredictable. One day I would be fine and the next day I'd be kicking, screaming and just plain lashing out. Centering me down and diffusing my tantrums took a great deal of patience.

This is where the "job" I mentioned before really kicked in. I started intensive speech, occupational and physical therapy for over thirteen years from ages four and a half to almost eighteen. Physical therapy was probably one of the most intense therapies for me because of another disability I have, dysgraphia, a handwriting disorder, which is an impairment of my writing ability caused by motor skill issues and the basic inability to hold a writing instrument.

While all these therapies were happening, my parents (without whom I wouldn't be here at this point) had also gotten me into theatre and as many extra-curricular activities as I could handle. When it came to transitioning, which many individuals with autism have difficulties with, their strategy was to face this head-on with as much scheduling and preparation before and after as possible.

You see autism can affect many people differently. Some of the most common characteristics of individuals with autism are honing in on a key interest to the exclusion of everything else at the time and repetitive behaviors. My parents challenged me to treat these symptoms as skills and make them into positives to help me advance. They truly worked off the mantra of turning my disability characteristics into abilities. My mom came up with so many different mantras towards helping me, but the main ones were:

"No Problems, Just Solutions"

"Trial and Error"

"The Three Trial Rule"

"Constraints and Opportunities"

"Abilities not disabilities"

These served me well growing up. After all the pee-wee sports programs, bowling, tennis, swimming, art courses, chess lessons, piano lessons, basketball camps, and after-school programs, I would find my niche in basketball and theatre. Basketball helped me finally make some friends with similar interests while theatre helped me build my communication skills. Twenty-one years later these two things are still my strongest passions in life.

I ended up playing basketball throughout high school and was varsity captain my senior year. While basketball ended for me in high school, I was still able to live one of my dreams while working on the NCAA March Madness Tournament during my junior year in college as an intern for CBS Sports. Today I continue to be a huge basketball junkie as a Seton Hall Alum with my Seton Hall Pirates and the NBA as a Los Angeles Lakers fan.

As for drama, I've been in more than twenty plays. One of those plays included a lead as Arthur (from the nationally acclaimed PBS series "Arthur") when I was in sixth grade. I also played the character of Ichabod Crane from "Sleepy Hollow" during my senior year in high school. As I did with basketball, I stopped performing after high school to focus on my studies but as a senior at Seton Hall, I received the amazing opportunity from producer Todd Graff to help with the motion picture *Joyful Noise*. I was a consultant for a character in the film who had Asperger syndrome! The movie premiered in Hollywood in January 2012 with my family and I in attendance.

While these two passions have certainly helped me along my way, a passion I found later is the reason why I'm writing this book today. After graduating high school, I received a partial scholarship from the Autism Society of America to attend college. I flew out to Arizona to their annual summer conference to receive the award. There I discovered the nuts and bolts of self-advocacy for the first time. There were countless individuals with autism there who wanted to share their experiences and help in the lives of others.

Serving the community around me has always been something I've held dear, and the chance to possibly help someone who has gone through a similar experience was an eye-opening revelation. After the conference, I decided to commit myself to autism advocacy by sharing my story, learning more about the autism community around me, and now expressing my heart in speeches and verses about autism.

I've been a self-advocate for the past six years and have worked with wonderful organizations such as Autism Speaks and the Autism Society of America. My efforts led me to receive a 5,000-dollar scholarship for graduate school from the National Speakers Association to pursue speaking as a career. I now go around the country as a National Motivational Speaker. In addition I discuss disabilities, overcoming obstacles, anti-bullying campaigns, and how to live life with a positive attitude.

I've also spent time as a consultant for parents with autistic children and as a freelance writer for many prominent publications. In the end, my life has been filled with many challenges but more recently also many successes along the way.

What I wanted to do with this book is to share with you a collection of pieces I've written over the years discussing autism from my heart. I've written a lot over the last few years, but these pieces have been the ones that have come to me effortlessly. They are the works I care about the most, because they were created not only in my brain but also from the raw emotion of my heart.

I hope this will help inspire those reading by showing that having autism can be different than the negative portrayal it sometimes gets in our society. Having autism may make a person appear different, but it absolutely **DOES NOT** make them any less of a person.

So without further ado, here is a piece of my heart in the works that have led me to this point in my journey so far…which needs to start with my mother.

A MOTHER'S INTRODUCTION

For several weeks, Kerry has been asking me to write an introduction to his e-book. It's not that I lacked the desire to assist, but when to find the time? We are busy at our house. We have always been busy at our house. A few weeks ago, Kerry graduated with a master's from Seton Hall University. He also received 501c3 approval for his company *KFM Making a Difference* from the IRS. He just completed reviewing applications for the second scholarship he set up for a student like himself who has autism. He just recently started his first full-time job in NYC. Four days into his job he was flying around the country to Little Rock, Arkansas to be the keynote speaker at the Arkansas Children's Hospital, *Team Up Autism* conference. Locally he continues doing events to raise autism awareness.

Last night I stayed up until he came in from dancing with friends. I assure you at age four I would not envision either his having friends or him being out by himself until 4 A.M. With familiarity that has come from two and a half decades of dealing with his autism, I can share what a joy he is.

I do what other mothers of typical children do everyday, but I also do what mothers of children on the spectrum do everyday. On a recent trip to Boston I met a mother of a four year old on the spectrum. When we talked the years faded away as the symptoms of her son and mine matched point on point and we talked strategies. I realized the journey for mothers of children on the spectrum today is very similar to my story. Mothers and children are walking in our footsteps. Hopefully Kerry sharing his/our story will help them and their children. We would both like that.

Today I am happy to read his book.

Kerry mentions his trip to Arizona in 2007 when he won the CVS *All Kids Can* scholarship from the Autism Society as a high school graduate. He credits his career as an Autism Advocate as beginning there. He is absolutely correct although neither of us knew it then. While Kerry and his dad slept in the first morning of the conference, I attended the opening session of the convention where the activities towards declaring United Nations Declaration of World Autism Awareness Day beginning on April 2, 2008 were highlighted.

In the presentation, the keynote speaker discussed his role in the autistic movement as the father of an autistic child. He remarked that the time was coming when the children that made up the autism community, the individuals that the entire movement of grandparents, parents, therapists, and countless professionals around the world were devoting their resources and passion to assist – that soon the time was at hand for those individuals were coming of age and would soon come to have their "voices" heard. Autistic individuals advocating for themselves and their community would forever change the autistic movement for the better. After the speech I bought Kerry a muffin and juice never thinking one of those autistic individuals he was talking about would be my son Kerry. I had no idea that in the near future Kerry would become a voice for the autistic community.

Two months later Kerry started Seton Hall University in South Orange, N.J. We had already made the painful decision (for us) to let him live on campus (he had never even been on a bus alone). I saw Kerry begin to find his voice and his role as an advocate when at Seton Hall he started a club celebrating student disabilities. It took a lot of courage to "out" his autism on a campus better known for basketball. More importantly the founding of Student Disability Awareness (SDA) started him on this current phase in his journey to make a difference in the lives of others in the autism community.

I realize this journey is still in the start up phase. Six years later Kerry Francis Magro, a remarkable young adult with autism, is recognized as one of the leading self-advocate voices in the autistic community. He has chosen to advocate for himself and those in his community, and they are so lucky to have him as one of their voices.

The question I ask myself when I travel with Kerry is: how did we get here? Some people question whether he has autism. He does. He was diagnosed for his accommodations for his Graduate Record Exams, GRE's two years ago. I write some of that in a Mother's Perspective later in this work. Most ask for something they can do to have a similar outcome for their child.

My best advice is to watch patiently and when you see a glimmer of interest in your child, run with it. For us I instilled in Kerry a deep sense of competition not with other children but within himself. He was always competing with that inner voice that didn't want to try anything; with that inner voice that would lead him to get past the epic melt downs we experienced if things even slightly changed his routines or didn't go precisely his way.

For us he would be recognized and rewarded for his trying something. Success was always defined by his participation, not how good he was at something. This worked for him when nothing else did. He would be recognized for his efforts and as a result I have a kid that will never say no to an opportunity. Those skills were honed at Seton Hall by Mike Reuter, Director of the Leadership Program in the Stillman School of Business. Mike simply taught everyone in his program that *they are the best of the best.* So while most of the class is off to careers in law and business Kerry seems to be heading in a direction to public service, public speaking and advocacy on behalf of his/our community.

In so many weeks that I have traveled around the country with him, and allowed him nervously to travel himself in the US and Canada, I have watched the faces of the parents and grandparents who hear his story. I have watched their response to his genuineness and the hope that he instills that their loved one will have as much success, and will have an independent life. I know what they hope for because twenty-one years ago I was hoping for the same thing for him, and I had no Kerry Magro as a beacon to show me the way.

Kerry gives to families what few others do: a view from someone who is autistic, a view from inside, and from his heart.

Kerry often says, **"Autism can't define me. I define autism."**

You do Kerry.

You define autism and from the bottom of my heart Kerry, I love you!

Autism is wonderful!

CHAPTER 1: MY NAME IS KERRY AND I HAVE PDD-NOS

My name is Kerry, and I have Pervasive Developmental Disorder-Not Otherwise Specified.

This means I have autism.

This does not mean I *am* autism.

This means I sometimes see the world in a different light.

This does not mean I'm in the dark.

This means from time to time I may have a difficulty expressing my emotions.

This does not mean I don't feel.

This means when I communicate, I do it with a style that is my own.

This does not mean I don't have a voice.

This means I may have sensitivity when it comes to a certain feel or touch.

This means sounds can sometimes make me feel uneasy.

This does not mean I'm deaf or hard of hearing.

This means I can often focus on certain interests for a long period of time.

This does not mean those are my only interests.

This means that I'm the only person in my family to have this.

This does not mean I'm alone.

This means I may have 500 other symptoms/capabilities that are different than yours.

This does not mean I'm any less a person than you are.

My name is Kerry, and regardless of what PDD-NOS means or doesn't mean, Autism can't define me; I define Autism.

I can only hope those individuals, regardless of being autistic or not, can define their lives and their journeys in the way they see it.

CHAPTER 2: ONLY IF YOU KNEW ME

If you knew me

You would know I was nonverbal at two-and-a-half.

You would know I was diagnosed with autism at four.

You would know I got kicked out of two preschools.

You would know I had extreme sensory integration difficulties.

You would know I would lash out to get attention when I couldn't communicate on my own.

You would know I twirled my hair.

You would know that when I was in school, my peers labeled special education "wrong" instead of "special".

You would know I spent hundreds of hours a year in therapy to get to where I am.

You would know I spent hundreds of hours being bullied because of my diagnosis.

You would know that being institutionalized was a possibility...

But if you also knew me...

You would know I graduated grade school.

You would know I graduated high school.

You would know I graduated college.

You would know I received my Master of Arts in Strategic Communication.

You would know I have a job.

You would know I live independently.

You would know I consult to help parents who have children with autism.

You would know I am a motivational speaker, life coach, and author.

You would know I have had a girlfriend.

You would know I love my family, my friends, and the autism community that is out there.

You would know that I'm Kerry and no matter what autism means or doesn't mean, I'm being the best me I can be…

Only if you knew me...

CHAPTER 3: THIS ONE'S FOR YOU

Yesterday was my graduation from Seton Hall University. As this has been one of the most emotional and happiest days of my life, I have taken some time to reflect on my journey and get my thoughts down on paper. Many people told me that my road towards a good education was going to be rough.

The word "impossible" was a word that I learned very early on in regard to people's opinions about whether or not I could get to college let alone graduate from college. Now I just have to say…

To the learning consultant that told me when I was six that I would be lucky to get to high school, this one's for you.

For the Special-Education teachers who would look down at me like I was broken, this one's for you.

For the years of being taunted and bullied by kids, saying I can't and wouldn't achieve greatness, this one's for you.

For the people who helped me through physical therapy, occupational therapy and speech therapy until I was fourteen, this one's for you.

For my parents, friends and relatives, who see me as an individual first who is/was never broken, this one's for you.

For those teachers who said, I could do it, this one's for you.

For the countless other individuals out there who are autistic or love someone who is autistic, this one's for you.

For the people who say you can't do something even though you can, this one's for you.

For the people at Autism Speaks who have given me the chance to express my "voice" and help others through the Autism Speaks Blog for over a year now, this one's for you.

At the end of the day our influences in our lives send us on our path, either good or bad. When I was four, I was diagnosed on the spectrum. Now twenty-one years later I'm am a college graduate and completed "With Distinction" my Master of Arts program in Strategic Communication. For all those people, again, the good and the bad, thank you. You've made me who I am today, and I wouldn't have it any other way.

…This one's for you.

CHAPTER 4: KEEP STRIVING

People religiously ask when they see me today what I did to get myself to the point I am at today. Many of the times it's parents with children who have just been recently diagnosed with autism.

And the answer most of the time is that if I've learned anything, it's that in this life you need to strive.

As an adult with autism I would think of myself sometimes in my mind looking into a mirror saying today:

You need to strive to better.

You need to strive to think smarter.

You need to strive to find your passions.

You need to strive to find your niche.

You need to strive if you want to get ahead.

You need to strive for progress.

This was a concept I look at today as second nature and early on that my parents tried to enforce in me. My parents strive to be better and work harder everyday.

When I was growing up...

They helped me strive for the right therapies.

They helped me strive for the right schools.

They helped me strive for the right diets.

They helped me strive for the best extra curricular activities.

They helped me strive to find my voice.

Each one of these individuals progress should always be the ultimate key to strive for. Have the plan, do the research and always strive for the best you. As the old saying goes, "no one can be a better you than you.

CHAPTER 5: RELATIONSHIPS: THE GOOD AND BAD WITH AUTISM

It's interesting to reflect on my life today and to think about relationships I've been in. I've been in relationships with girls who have both had a disability and who have not. It's also interesting to look at how my relationships have evolved since I've been a self-advocate for autism.

Some of the relationships have been good.

Some of the relationships have been bad.

And then some of the relationships have just been so confusing I couldn't tell good from bad.

For those looking for love in today's world what I can tell you from my personal experience is that you always have to take the individual first and then take the rest of the baggage after it. We all end up having some baggage due to our past experiences.

Confused yet? Well, what I mean to say is that you have to look at me as Kerry first and then weigh in what autism means to how you portray me once you get to know me.

Don't see my autism as baggage but a way to learn about someone differently. If you are looking at an autism characteristic try to learn the story behind that.

So again,

Some of my relationships have been good.

Some of them have been bad.

But in the end, you lose out by not taking the time to look at the whole package. Give us time and we may very well surprise you.

Remember, everyone deserves to be loved…

.

CHAPTER 6: THE #1 UNIVERSAL AUTISM TREATMENTS

These days Autism's treatments/therapies are always discussed. Some work, some don't and many times it's just hit and miss based on the specific individual and where they are on the spectrum. Autism is a *huge* spectrum (with people ranging from low functioning to high functioning, some nonverbal, some with communication difficulties; some have speech but social interaction/integration difficulties).

One thing I think must be considered above everything else, though, is a treatment that never runs out of demand and is free.

This treatment will make sure your days are beyond special, and that starts with....

Unconditional Love.

Love makes us understand we are special.

Love makes it so we can go through our days with someone.

Love means we can wake up each day with a sense of comfort.

You may not see it in some of us at times, but inside it can make a huge impact.

Love makes having whatever autistic characteristics you may have ok.

Because you have love.

You have someone who loves you for you.

This is why the best way to help an individual with autism will always start with unconditional love and acceptance.

It's the universal treatment that we will always want and need.

CHAPTER 7: WHEN I FIRST UNDERSTOOD I HAD AUTISM

"You have autism."

The doctor said that when I was four and a half.

"You have autism." What that was I had no idea.

The tribulations would drive my parents and myself nuts at times.

"You have autism."

It was something that was unknown to me for the next seven years.

Then I understood the word autism.

At eleven and a half, I began to question why I was in a Special Ed setting. Why was I going to a school where everyone had a learning disability and what did having a learning disability even mean?

The first teacher I asked about it told me I was there because of some of my social difficulties. Then I asked my parents, and they explained to me what autism was. I wasn't sure at first if it had something to do with my dysgraphia because I certainly knew I wasn't artistic. Then I only…

understood the "label" of autism. Mine was PDD-NOS.

The specifics would come together a few years later but the main thing that happened was I found out about the characteristics.

I started noticing the communication and social interaction difficulties some had.

Then I started processing it and applying it to who I was and what it meant in my life. During the entire time, I kept asking questions to better understand autism.

Today I understand autism, for the most part. I understand how it applies to who I am but my wish is for us to keep learning more and more about the nuts and bolts of autism. Things like what causes autism, how did it come about, why the dramatic rise?

My message though for those individuals who are first learning about having autism or telling someone about autism is that you always keep the love in the room. The main thing is that autism isn't a disease. It's not a death sentence, and therefore, it shouldn't be treated as such. Know that it is a disability but many individuals with disabilities live very rewarding lives.

So I would say you need to first understand that it's about loving who you are and your loved ones. It must be an authentic love and when it is, it will make a world of difference.

CHAPTER 8: TELLING MY PAST SELF ABOUT MY DOUBTS OF COMING OUT

This is me thinking to myself then when deciding to tell people about having autism...

What if they don't like me?

What if they don't understand me?

What if they see me as damaged?

What if they see me as wrong?

What if they don't like some of my traits?

What if I can't make people understand that it's a part of me?

If I could go back and talk to my past self, I would say...

I do like you.

I do understand you.

You are not damaged and aren't less.

You are as right as anyone can be in the world.

If I don't like your traits when first seeing them, I would understand its part of what makes you who you are.

Lastly, there will always be people who don't understand and don't want to understand. You as an individual though shouldn't fear that people won't understand the type of person you are because understanding comes with how you understand yourself first. Reflecting on who you are and understanding that is so essential in this life.

So Kerry, remember, autism or not you can't have your voice taken away by anyone else but yourself. Be proud of who you are and cherish the uniqueness that comes with you because that's what you will carry with you for your entire life. Love yourself and let those people who do understand you love you for who you are.

If you do all of these things, everything will be ok. The future is bright for you Kerry, and you will see that soon.

CHAPTER 9: PROVE THEM WRONG

I have a story to share with you today...

So...

I was born January 15, 1988 in New York, New York. My parents named me Kerry Francis Magro.

When I was four...I was diagnosed with something called...

Autism...

Autism is a communication and social interaction disorder...

Today it affects one in every eighty-eight children...

Back when I was diagnosed very little known was known about autism...

Growing up was tough...

Between motor skill issues...

Auditory processing issues…

Speech issues…

Sensory integration dysfunction issues…

And difficulties interacting with others…

Many people weren't giving me a shot to live what many call a "Normal Life."

Like getting a job…

Or even to live by myself one-day…

I did something, which many thought I couldn't…

I proved them wrong…

I graduated from high school…

I graduated from college at Seton Hall University…

I even have had jobs such as…

A photographer…

A researcher…

A social media consultant for Autism Speaks…

And much more!

Today…

I consult for parents who have children with autism…

I still work for Autism Speaks…

I'm writing a book about my college experience…

So the next time someone says you or a loved one can't do something…

Smile…

Sure some of us may have limitations…

All of us have some difficulties…

But through a positive attitude…

And having a passion for what you're doing…

We can do amazing and unique things in this world…

It is not in one of us, but it's in all of us…

Believe in a better future today and I promise you an eternity of happiness…

So again, autism or not…

Prove them wrong. And remember that no matter how dark life gets sometimes…

You are not alone

CHAPTER 10: SPREADING THE WORD

I have a question for you today…

Who do you call retarded?

Is it someone who is mentally retarded?

Maybe people with developmental disabilities?

The eleven-year-old who is nonverbal?

The five-year-old with Attention Deficit Disorder?

How about the kid who takes possibly longer to read than others due to Dyslexia?

But why stop there…?

How about someone with Alzheimer's who can barely remember their name?

Or someone with a Bipolar Disorder or Obsessive Compulsive Disorder?

What about someone suffering from a traumatic brain injury?

How about your friend who may not have a disability?

You might just use a term such as "wow-you're so retarded sometimes" to a friend.

The problem is today that every time you use the word retarded you help give it a voice.

Most of the time the word is used in a way to be hurtful to others.

The more power we give to the word around the world, the more chance it will be used to insult others.

I can attest to this. I was diagnosed with autism when I was four years old. Being in Special-Education classes for most of my life, the word retarded was thrown around to insult me. Many times I was defeated because of this. Not only classmates, but also kids outside of our classes would call us the "retarded class" because they knew we were special education.

At the end of the day all of us deserve to be treated as people with respect. Together we should stop using the word retard and make a difference in the lives of those with disabilities.

Every first Wednesday in March we spread awareness through a campaign called "Spread the Word to End the Word" to help the millions of disabled individuals around the country.

This is me speaking at a Project Unify "Spread the Word to End the Word" event in my hometown of Jersey City. (Shout out to Dr. Gerry Crisonino!)

So in closing I ask you to do this...

Be educated

Learn the facts

And please be understanding of others

As a society... we will be a whole lot better for it

PHOTOS: MY JOURNEY TILL NOW

BORN JANUARY 15, 1988…

I WAS FIRST DIAGNOSED WITH AUTISM AT 4…

GROWING UP WAS DEFINITELY TOUGH.
HAVING LIMITED SPEECH EARLY ON MADE IT
TOUGH TO KEEP UP WITH MY PEERS. MIX THAT
WITH SENSORY ISSUES, TWIRLING, LIMITED
PLAY, ALONG WITH MOTOR ISSUES, AND IT WAS
TOUGH ON MYSELF AND ON MY FAMILY.

AS YOU WILL SEE IN THE BOOK THOUGH MY
PARENTS WOULDN'T STOP AND NEITHER CAN
THE PARENTS WHO ARE READING THIS TODAY
TO HELP THEIR LOVED ONES. MY PARENTS
WERE ABLE TO MAKE TREMENDOUS STRIDES
FOR ME. ONE THING THAT HELPED ME ALONG
WITH PHYSICAL THERAPY, OCCUPATIONAL
THERAPY, SPEECH THERAPY, AND HOURS OF
ONE ON ONE TUTORING WAS STICKING TO MY
PASSIONS…
FOR EXAMPLE…

ONE OF THE BIGGEST PASSIONS IN MY LIFE IS
BASKETBALL. MY OBSESSION HAS BEEN SO BAD
WE'VE GONE OUT TO SEE MY FAVORITE TEAM
THE LAKERS PLAY ON CHRISTMAS TWICE IN
THE PAST FIVE YEARS. THIS WAS A PHOTO
FROM A LAKERS VS. CELTICS GAME ME AND MY
PARENTS WENT A FEW YEARS AGO.

THE STORY BEHIND BASKETBALL IS AN
INTERESTING ONE. WHEN I WAS IN HIGH
SCHOOL I WAS 230 POUNDS BUT BECAUSE OF MY
LOVE FOR BASKETBALL I WANTED TO MAKE
MY HIGH SCHOOL TEAM. I DIDN'T MY
FRESHMAN YEAR BUT LOST 60 POUNDS THAT
SUMMER, MADE JV MY SOPHOMORE YEAR,
VARISTY JUNIOR YEAR AND WAS VARSITY
CAPTAIN SENIOR YEAR! IT SHOWED ME THAT
HARD WORK CAN PAY OFF!

MY OTHER PASSION WILL ALWAYS BE THEATER.
THEATER MADE A BIG DIFFERENCE IN MY
EARLY DEVELOPMENT. I WAS ALWAYS A FAN OF
MUSIC BUT NEVER HAD MUCH RHYTHM OR
SINGING ABILITY. WE TURNED MY LOVE OF
MUSICAL THEATER INTO MORE DRAMATIC
ACTING WHICH LED ME TO BEING IN OVER 20
PLAYS IN MY LIFE OVER 12 YEARS…

I EVEN CONSULTED FOR A MOTION PICTURE
CALLED *JOYFUL NOISE* FOR A CHARACTER WHO
HAD ASPERGER SYNDROME IN THE FILM!

FINALLY, ONE OF MY BIGGEST PASSIONS WAS GETTING THROUGH SCHOOL. REGARDLESS OF MY DIFFICULTIES…I WAS ABLE TO GRADUATE FROM GRADE SCHOOL, HIGH SCHOOL AND COLLEGE…

AND... MOST RECENTLY GRADUATING WITH MY MASTER'S!

TODAY I DO MANY THINGS INCLUDING
SPEAKING. THIS PICTURE IS FROM MY FIRST
MOTIVATIONAL SPEAKING EVENT WHICH LED
TO A PARTIAL SCHOLARSHIP FROM THE
NATIONAL SPEAKERS ASSOCIATION FOR
GRADUATE SCHOOL.

I CAN'T WAIT TO SEE WHAT THE FUTURE HAS IN
STORE FOR ME NEXT! THIS JOURNEY IS
SOMETHING I'M REALLY LOOKING FORWARD
TO.

WITHOUT FURTHER ADO WE BRING YOU BACK
TO YOUR SCHEDULED PROGRAMMING WITH A
REFLECTION ON MY LIFE IN COLLEGE

**P.S: IT'S NOT THE STORY OF ME STAYING UP
TILL 4 AM CAUSING SHENANIGANS! THAT'S A
STORY FOR THE NEXT BOOK ABOUT MY
COLLEGE EXPERIENCE! STAY TUNED FOR
THAT! ☺**

CHAPTER 11: SELF REFLECTION: MY LIFE IN COLLEGE

Being able to live life in self-reflection…

I connected to this concept right away and I still do it till this day. No matter what my day looks like, I take a few minutes at the beginning of the day, the middle of my day and at the end of my day to reflect on anything and everything going around me. In college, whenever I finished a project or semester, I did the same reflection just for longer periods.

One of my biggest strengths is my love of typing. When I was a kid, because of my motor skill issues I had always used a keyboard. Growing up computers were a key interest for me. Because of this when I was in college I would usually keep a daily journal of all my events and write them down in an excel spreadsheet to keep track of everything that was going on. Something that has been instrumental in writing my first book!

10 things I've learned about myself…

Autism can't define me, only I can define autism.

Give advice to others in the autistic community through your own experiences.

If someone calls you "awkward," just know that it means you're "unique" and a lot better than "ordinary".

I'm great at several things and broken in none.

Ignorance is all around us but awareness is around the corner if we want it to be.

Feeling sorry for myself will get me nowhere.

We need to stop labeling and instead integrate, "people with people" in our communities who have different needs.

Inclusion in schools will never mean I'm secluded from an education.

Autism is not a disease, rather a disability that every day I strive to become an ability.

Communication never takes a vacation so neither can I.

The last one here is probably the one that holds the most impact to my learning of autism in college. It holds the most impact mainly because I was, for a time in my life, nonverbal. I was two and a half years old and had no speech whatsoever. Even though I began saying words just a little time later it was a difficult road trying to put a lot of the pieces into the puzzle. I can remember at an early age having the words in my head but not being able to put the words together to form sentences and beyond was always a challenge.

I can honestly say when I look at where I've come from since it still feels like a dream. Getting a master's degree in communications, which used to be one of my greatest weaknesses is crazy to me now. I will continue to pursue communication and learning more and more about it because I know I have a long way to go but I'm ready for it! Can't wait.

CHAPTER 12: WILL HE EVER SPEAK?

I wanted to share an experience I had which perfectly reflects why I speak out for individuals on the spectrum. It all started off in May 2011 when a woman approached me after speaking at the Municipal Chambers in Jersey City, New Jersey for an Autism Awareness event. I was the keynote speaker. After speaking she introduced herself and told me she desperately needed my help. It was a memory, which still sticks out to me to this day.

Standing there, the woman asked, "My five-year-old son was just diagnosed with PDD-NOS and has no speech. Will he ever be able to speak?"

While the young mother stood before me in tears, I felt trapped. Trapped because I couldn't tell her that everything was going to be all right.

When I look back at my life, that 6-year-old boy, going into first grade with so much anger, and so many emotions, it was almost too much. I knew back then I was mad. I was lashing out because I didn't know how to communicate in an appropriate manner. That was almost 19 years ago. I was that six-year-old again. What would it take for her son to be able to speak one day? Would he be as lucky as me?

So, I surprised myself. I hugged her. I hugged this complete stranger for what probably ended up being five minutes. No words were said. I could only hear her sobbing and I almost joined her several times. I knew I couldn't answer her question, but by telling her about my journey, I could give her hope.

I reflected back to the journey that led me to where I am today. The therapies, the special need classrooms, the accommodations, the hate, the ignorance, the awareness, the drama, the acceptance, the struggle, the tears, the heartache, the strength, the friends, my mom, my dad, and above all else the love that has made my journey worth every second. After we hugged I told her my story. I told her about that six year-old boy and how he became who I was today. 15 minutes later tears of uncertainty had become tears of hope for not only her but for her son.

This is why I speak. Each time I share my story I pray that I'm making an impact on a parent, a family, a friend, for the future of the autism movement. I may not be a scientist, or an expert in the field, I just know what it's like to grow up–and thrive with autism.

So, if you have autism, especially those young adults out there who are trying to spread awareness at the college level or beyond, tell your story. The world has so much to learn from us.

CHAPTER 13: A MOTHER'S PERSPECTIVE FROM THE HEART

Looking at Kerry today I wish twenty-one years ago someone offered me the inspiration and hope that he represents, and I can see why anyone would ask the question, of how he got to where he is today. His PDD-NOS was severe. Although we did not know what PDD NOS was, they mentioned that some children were institutionalized and that's all I heard.

Kerry was our delightful only child reaching most development (height, weight) milestones except speech until he was two and a half years old. At two and a half, he started to show extreme signs of sensory integration dysfunction. He was afraid of a wide variety of things because of sensory issues. Wind, rain, water, and noises loud and soft were major problems.

There was a time when we could not bathe him - uneven surfaces such as sand and or swings where he couldn't feel the bottom below him were a problem. He was asked to leave two different pre schools, because they couldn't handle him. Later he preferred isolation, would not interact or participate with other children. He had delayed speech, limited pretend play, echolalia- repeating things, twirled around, flapping when he was upset, extreme difficulty with transitions and tantrums. He had fine and gross motor delays.

When I dropped him off in the morning, at day-care he would scream he didn't want to go in, and when I picked him up in the afternoon, I would have to drag him screaming, because he didn't want to leave. Once home with a caregiver he would scream at the top of the stairs, "Go away."

Kerry was diagnosed first by Hackensack Hospital and then by Doctor Margaret Hertzig, the Director of Pediatric Psychiatry at Cornell. Doctor Hertzig is a world-renowned expert in Autistic and Autism-Spectrum Disorders. She saw him as he grew marking the improvement she saw. Interestingly to us she reconfirmed Kerry's diagnosis for his accommodations for the GRE's a few years ago as he started graduate school.

The Kerry you see today is not the Kerry I watched grow up   Kerry did not come together for many years. After his diagnosis, finally, we tried to get him into a pre school handicapped class. There was a delay, so we began Occupational Therapy (OT) at home with Robert Sheppard, OTR, and a Pediatric OT working on the Sensory Integration Dysfunction (SID) issues as well as speech. OT continued at home until he was seven as well as in school where he was in a multi-handicapped class receiving speech, and OT. At seven he began intensive work surrounding Physical Therapy (PT) and OT therapy at Hackensack Hospital with Jude Riekert, OTR, where he did a lot of work with vestibular planning exercises. He is seen privately to this day for OT/PT as needed by a local PT.

One of the major things that worked for us was sports. Although he did not want to be around people, I got him involved in peewee bowling, and then sent him to the Jewish Community Center (JCC) on the Palisades in Tenafly, New Jersey. Their summer program, Camp Tikvah was for children with neurological issues. The camp was wonderful in that they did a different activity every forty minutes, and the forced transitions helped condition him. The vestibular planning therapy he was having also helped with sensory, balance, speech, and language development.

Kerry started to respond to recognition; praise, rewards and I ran with that. We have a million great job stickers, magnets and trophies. I developed my own token economy barter system. If he tried something three times, he would get a predetermined reward (seeing a movie, an action figure, games, another great job sticker) that we agreed on.

If after the third time he did not want to do something, I would agree to let him drop it. Since he wanted to do nothing, three times sometimes seemed interminable for both of us, but I kept to it and found a kid who loves bowling, played soccer, and basketball. T-Ball was rougher with the coordination issues and was dropped, but not until the third season.

All this time, speech, physical and occupational therapies continued. We started to look to things that didn't require group interaction but that he might get good at and enjoy. That led us to piano lessons with Carl Botti to improve his co-ordination and motor dexterity. We hired Bobby Stewart to teach Kerry chess to help him with critical thinking.

I am often asked how Kerry became the self assured man he is today. Regrettably I don't have the prescription and we had no idea it would be better until it was.

I do know no matter what I'll always love Kerry for who he is. It's so important for other parents to remember to do the same for their loved ones.

Of note on the page long list of diagnoses in 1992 there was one for me, Parent/Child problem. They noted in the report that they did not believe I would ever accept his diagnosis – I proved them wrong! I embraced his autism with every hug and good job sticker!

(I wanted to thank Joe Panepinto, who recommended Camp Tikvah, because his daughter Roseanne was a camp counselor at JCC. This one's for you Joe!)

CHAPTER 14: TEACHING PEOPLE THAT AUTISM DOESN'T MAKE YOU HARMFUL

The Sandy Hook Elementary shootings changed everything. We realized there were things that needed to be changed…

One thing that changed for many in the autism community, though, was how we were viewed. The shooter was believed to have Asperger's syndrome, a form of autism and many people took this to believe that the majority of us were dangerous. As time has gone by this type of buzz has passed but there are still hate groups that think the world would be better without us.

This is something that is completely untrue of many others and me. I wrote a letter to the media outlets expressing my emotions when this happened, which read…

Dear Media Outlets, Everywhere,

As we mourn for the victims in the shooting at Sandy Hook Elementary School, please refrain from doing damage to our community by linking autism with violence.

Even if we find out that the shooter did, in fact, have autism it does not mean our community is dangerous as we are more likely to have someone commit a violent crime towards us than the other way around.

Many people already see autism as 'wrong' and these false reports will lead to nothing but further ignorance for countless individuals who more than anything want to be accepted for who they are.

Please say you'll try to understand…

Warm Regards,

A (Non-Violent) Autistic Adult

I posted this on Facebook not knowing what to expect or if anyone would respond at all. Today, this letter has over 490 likes and 2,440 shares on Facebook! This made me tear up a bit because while all of this was going on my Grandma passed away the week before from a fifteen yearlong battle with Alzheimer's disease. It made me realize that there were still people out there who were good and loved autistic individuals.

It was a reminder that even though we must push acceptance in our society, for some at least there were still some people out there who already grasped how great autistic people are and can be. What a feeling…

Later I would learn that two of the children murdered that day were part of our autistic community; Dylan Hockley 6, and Josephine " Joey " Gay 7, who was non-verbal. To their parents and all of the victims families take solace in knowing your children knew they were truly loved everyday.

CHAPTER 15: A TESTIMONY FOR CHANGE

This was the speech I wrote when I testified in front of The Department of Health and Human Services Committee in New York about including services for autistic individuals under the Patient Protection and Affordable Care Act in November 2011. Advocacy has become a huge interest for me in terms of health care reform. In particular, I worked closely with Senator Robert Menendez, NJ, on the Combating Autism Reauthorization (CARA) Act in 2011 to help give government funding to Autism research. Hope you enjoy this.

When I was four, I was diagnosed with autism.

Growing up, people would always tell me what my future was; and that future certainly did not involve being here speaking to you all today.

I was lucky. I had a great health-care plan. My family spent countless hours to make sure I would get the services I needed and with a little luck, I was put on the path to have all my dreams come true.

This is why I'm here today. No matter if it's Applied Behavior Analysis, (ABA) Speech Therapy, Occupational Therapy, Physical Therapy, we all have a chance to strive with the right services. Today we have over twenty-nine states with some form of autism legislation put in place. This wasn't done by magic but by hard-working citizens much like the people in this room who are here simply because we have voices that want to be heard for a better day.

In addition, this is why I speak at events such as this; I speak because I envision a future where all my autistic brothers and sisters don't have to worry about communication and social deficiencies. I envision a day where my friend can speak to her autistic cousin without having to cry because he won't speak back. I envision a day where I can go to my hometown and see my eight-year-old Mentee surrounded by countless friends at his birthday party. The good news is this day could very well be possible for some. In today's society, autism is becoming much more treatable and people are receiving the health care needed to live fully capable and independent lives.

If we want this progress to continue though, we need to keep making a difference when it comes to autism legislation. I've always stressed that we must turn all disabilities into abilities, especially autism, so we can therefore make a difference in our lives and the lives of others. If I can speak here today, as an adult with autism who was provided similar services to make speaking here even possible, imagine what it could look like for the future individuals with autism if given the right funding. Keep making a difference by including these services in our health benefits. Thank you.

After I spoke I was stunned to receive a standing ovation for my comments, and it led me to speak my heart much more often. I didn't feel defeated as I sometimes feel when speaking in front of crowds and actually felt accepted instead. It was one of the first, but certainly not the last, testimonies I would offer in the future.

CHAPTER 16: SEVENTEEN WISHES FROM AN ADULT WITH AUTISM

I wish that acceptance was easier to come by.

I wish that loving one another was always on our mind.

I wish that an "early diagnosis" remains a high priority.

I wish that people would stop calling autism a disease.

I wish that communication becomes easier for everyone with autism. We are trying.

I wish that we find more treatments to enhance the lives of people with autism.

I wish that insurance for autism gets passed in all 50 states.

I wish that the government would understand the need for services for the autistic in schools.

I wish that autistic individuals can one day live their lives independently.

I wish that I was capable of helping more.

I wish that people would stop using the words "socially awkward" and "retard" in a negative way.

I wish we raise awareness for all with disabilities. Those of us living with a disability are doing our very best.

I wish for those who are or love someone who is on the spectrum that you know that we are moving forward every single day.

I wish that all of our voices can be heard

I wish everyone will follow the words of one of my favorite performers of all time, Michael Jackson, who sang in his song called, "Man in the Mirror"...*If you want to make the world a better place, take a look at yourself and make a change.*

I wish you all knew me when I was four, when I was diagnosed with autism. For a long time, I was lost. Scared of myself and what I was capable of. I never thought I would be where I am today...but I did it. I graduated with departmental honors from Seton Hall University as an undergraduate and went on to graduate and get my Master degree in Strategic Communications with distinction.

So for my final wish...

I wish for you all to always live life with hope. I wish that your days are filled with hope for a better tomorrow, and for today no matter how dark life gets sometimes that you realize you're never alone.

I wish this for you…

CHAPTER 17: WHEN PEOPLE ASSUMED YOU'VE RECOVERED FROM AUTISM

Autism is a lifelong condition…. so why do people keep coming up to me saying I've recovered?

Many people who come up to me ask me how I have not only recovered but how I've been "cured" of autism.

It's never been that simple…

You see, behind the scenes I still deal with hypersensitivity.

Behind the scenes, I still deal with retention issues.

Behind the scenes, I still have a hard time with pronunciation and reading.

Behind the scenes, I still jump when someone tries to sneak up and touch me.

Behind the scenes, I still need therapy at times to deal with motor skills.

Behind the scenes, I'm still striving to progress as Kerry.

Behind the scenes, I'm still searching for ways to make myself better.

Behind the scenes, I am an autistic individual.

Behind the scenes, I haven't outgrown autism.

Behind the scenes, I haven't recovered from autism.

Behind the scenes, I haven't been cured from autism.

Because you haven't seen behind the scenes, you haven't seen the complete me. You haven't seen some of my struggles.

Can I speak pretty well and interact with others…Sure.

But that is on the surface. You don't know what happens behind the scenes. That's what I want you all to know. If you can't see something on the surface when you first meet me or frankly, anyone else you shouldn't expect that they don't struggle with a few things. I struggle with a lot of things, and I'm sure those of you reading this do as well.

So the next time you see me as "recovered" or that I've "outgrown autism," please remember not to speculate on all of that until you fully know the entire picture.

You could be doing more damage than you know.

CHAPTER 18: LOVING YOURSELF FOR YOU

This book was fashioned by love. What I hope I left you with is something that will inspire you. You see I have found in my life that getting down on myself was never the answer to a problem. I had to rise above and see myself as someone who was someone of value, and because of the love my parents had for me, I could do this.

Our society is constantly changing. As individuals we may switch our opinions of things but it's so important that we never change what we believe in.

As a kid I could never accept who I was.

As an adult, I hope everyone reading this knows that there is hope...

There will be struggles along the way as we progress and evolve, but it's important to remember to accept yourself for who you are and to love yourself for who you are.

Regardless if it's autism, another disability or another obstacle, anything really, the advice I can give is to never underestimate yourself and what you can do. Build off your strengths but also build on being comfortable in your own skin.

So parents, self-advocates, experts and readers, please remember…

"Loving yourself for you" is how we give permission for ourselves to love others and to go out into this world to do amazing things. It's what we need right now and what we will need in the future.

Nothing will or could ever beat love.

I wish you all a never-ending abundance of happiness in your lives.

Everyday can be a blessing with our loved ones so please let it be…

My name is Kerry...

And this is me defining autism from my heart...

ABOUT THE AUTHOR

Award Winning, Breakthrough Autism Self-Advocate Kerry Magro knew early on that he wanted to make a difference in the lives of others. Kerry was diagnosed with Pervasive Developmental Disorder-Not Otherwise Specified (PDD-NOS) at age four. Growing up, he dealt with many difficulties in regard to sensory integration, motor problems, and overall social interaction and communication delays. After being re-diagnosed at five, Kerry's future was very uncertain.

Today, however, after countless hours of therapy and the support of a loving family, Kerry has conquered many of his challenges. Now twenty-five years old, he is a recent master's graduate in Strategic Communications at Seton Hall University. Along with his master's, Kerry is a columnist at Autism After 16, a life coach, motivational speaker, writes a personal blog called My Autism My Voice, and is a consultant for individuals on the spectrum.

During this time he has also become a tireless advocate for students with disabilities around the state and nationally. He has appeared on Emmy-Winner Steve Adubato's Caucus Education Show, "One-on-One with Steve Adubato," has been published in the San Francisco Chronicle and serves as an advisor on the movie *Joyful Noise* starring Queen Latifah and Dolly Parton. Kerry in his advocacy work went to the Capital to meet with Senator Robert Menendez to discuss the Combating Autism Reauthorization Act of 2011.

SPECIAL THANKS TO SOME AMAZING PEOPLE...

David Chioda, my godfather.

Robert A. Sheppard and Jude Riekert, OTR

Claire Hurley, Family Fun Bowling League

Mrs. Barbara Balsamo Bogdanski - Kindergarten -First Grade Teacher

The Hazlet's, Jersey City Soccer Association

Joseph Panepinto

Staff - Camp Tikvah, & Center Stage, JCC on the Palisades, Tenafly, NJ

Carl Botti, Piano Teacher, Jersey City Public Schools

Bobby Stewart, Kings Knight Chess Club, Chess Coach

The Staff of Strulowitz and Gargiulo PT

Staff and Classmates of Community Lower School, Teaneck, NJ

Staff and Classmates of Community High School, Teaneck, NJ

Vincent Varrassi, MA. – College bound Coach,
www.vincentvarrassi.com

Student Disability Awareness, Seton Hall University

Alpha Phi Omega, Seton Hall University

Michael Reuter M.B.A., Director, Leadership Program, and
the Stillman School of Business, Seton Hall University

Senator Robert Menendez, New Jersey

Pat Kemp, Marc Sirkin, Bill Shea, Dana Marnane and everyone at
Autism Speaks!

Strategic Communication Department, Seton Hall University

Dr. Scott Herbert, Seton Hall University

Todd Graff, Director, *Joyful Noise*

RECOMMENDED SOURCES FOR MORE ON AUTISM...

My Autism My Voice- http://MyAutismMyVoice.com

Laura Shumaker: SF Gate- http://blog.sfgate.com/lshumaker/

Lou's Land- http://lous-land.blogspot.com/

Thinking Person's Guide to Autism-
http://www.thinkingautismguide.com/

A Diary of a Mom- http://adiaryofamom.wordpress.com/

ThAutcast- http://thautcast.com/drupal5/

Autism Speaks- http://www.autismspeaks.org/

Autism Society- http://www.autism-society.org/

Autism After 16- http://www.autismafter16.com/

A Wish Come Clear- http://awishcomeclear.com/

SQUAG- http://www.squag.com/

John Elder Robison: Look Me in The Eye- http://jerobison.blogspot.com/

Interactive Autism Network- http://www.ianproject.org/

Wrong Planet- http://www.wrongplanet.net/

Autism with a side of fries- http://autismwithasideoffries.blogspot.com/

Stuart Duncan- http://www.stuartduncan.name/

Squidalicious- http://www.squidalicious.com/

Big Daddy Autism- http://bigdaddyautism.com/

HAVE QUESTIONS?

I know there are many within our autism community struggling. For the future I hope to continue writing and helping others accept themselves for who they are. This will be one of my missions in a Non-Profit I've launched called "KFM Making A Difference."

One way I'm helping right now is through a scholarship program ran through this organization for young adults on the spectrum who are pursuing college called "Making A Difference For Autism Scholarship Program". In addition, my long-term goal is to start establishing affordable housing units to help adults with autism live independently. You can learn more about this by visiting my website at
www.kerrymagro.com

If you ever have a question or would just like to chat I frequently respond to people through my fan page on Facebook at…

www.facebook.com/kerrymagro88 and Twitter @Kerrymagro

If you ever have an inquiry or would like to submit a scheduling request to have me speak at your next event please feel free to reach out to me at…

kfmmakingadifference@gmail.com.

I already am working on several books, which I will hopefully have out in the next few years! If you ever have a story you want to share don't hesitate to contact me!